Cub Saves the Day

by Ann M. Rossi
illustrated by Costanza Basaluzzo

 HOUGHTON MIFFLIN HARCOURT
School Publishers

Copyright © by Houghton Mifflin Harcourt Publishing Company

Printed in China

ISBN-13: 978-0-547-02562-9
ISBN-10: 0-547-02562-9

3 4 5 6 7 8 0940 18 17 16 15 14 13 12 11 10

It was a fun day.
The class was finding out
how to be safe at school!

"Don't push at the water fountain,"
said the teacher.
"Don't swim in the water,"
said the teacher.

Water fountain

Cub helped Tadpole drink.
"When I grow up,
I won't need help,"
said Tadpole.

Tadpole

"Don't yell during lunch,"
said the teacher.
"And don't eat food from the floor.
It could be rotten!"

A breeze blew into the classroom.
It spilled Cub's honey on the floor.
"Oh, no," said Cub.

Insects running

The insects ran to
the puddle of honey.
"Don't run," said the teacher.
But the insects didn't listen.

Jar of honey

7

Cub started yelling,
"Stop, you'll get stuck!"

Cub yelling

8

His voice was very loud.

The insects started to cry.

The teacher came over.

Insects crying

"I didn't want to scare you.
I wanted you to be safe,"
said cub.
"You did the right thing,"
the teacher said.
"Thanks, Cub!" said the insects.

Responding

TARGET SKILL **Cause and Effect**

What happens in this story? Copy the chart below. Fill in the event that causes Cub to yell.

Causes	Effects
The wind blows.	Honey spills.
?	Cub yells.

Write About It

Text to Self Think about a time when you helped someone. Write a few sentences about what happened. Make sure that all your sentences are about what you helped someone do.

breeze	rotten
dangerous	scare
fountain	screaming
insects	sticky
judge	

✓ **TARGET SKILL** **Cause and Effect** Tell how one event makes another happen.

✓ **TARGET STRATEGY** **Summarize** Stop to tell important events as you read.

GENRE **Humorous fiction** is a story that is written to make the reader laugh.